RETURNS	Items must be returned or renewed on or before closing time on the last date marked above
RENEWALS	Unless required by other members, items may be renewed at the loaning library in person, or by post or telephone, on two occasions only.
INFORMATION NEEDED:	Member's card number.
MEMBERSHIP	Please notify any change of name or address.
STOCK CARE	Please look after this item. You may be charged for any damage.

Library of Congress Cataloging-in-Publication Data

Cohen-Posey, Kate.
   How to handle bullies, teasers, and other meanies : a book that
takes the nuisance out of name calling and other nonsense / by Kate
Cohen-Posey.
         p.   cm.
   Summary : Provides information on what makes bullies and teasers
tick, how to handle bullies, how to deal with prejudice, and how to
defend onesself when being teased or insulted.
   ISBN 1-56825-029-0
   1. Bullying--Juvenile literature.   2. Verbal self-defense--Juvenile
literature. [1. Bullying. 2] Bullies. 3. Self -defense.] I. Title.
BF637.B85C64   1995
646.7'0083--dc20   95-9191
                                                                CIP
                                                                 AC

How to Handle Bullies, Teasers, and Other Meanies:
A Book that Takes the Nuisance Out of
Name Calling and Other Nonsense
by Kate Cohen-Posey, M.S., LMHC, LMFT

Cover Design:	Kate Cohen-Posey and Betsy A. Lampé
Illustrations:	Betsy A. Lampé
Interior Design:	Virginia Condello
Retail Price:	$8.95
ISBN:	1-56825-029-0
Published by:	Rainbow Books, Inc.
	P. O. Box 430
	Highland City, FL 33846-0430
	Telephone: (863) 648-4420
	Email: RBIbooks@aol.com

Manufactured in the United States of America.

Dedication

This book is dedicated to all the young people who squeeze sweet juice from bitter fruit,
and
to any others who dare to learn!

The ideas in *How To Handle Bullies, Teasers And Other Meanies* apply to painful but harmless name calling. For more dangerous situations, other strategies may be needed. This material is offered as general information only. Readers are encouraged to seek advice about specific problems from qualified professionals.

Contents

NOTE TO PARENTS AND OTHER ADULTS: At times the language in this book is ugly because "ugly" is the language of bullies and teasers.

Introduction

Animals can only fight or flee —
because you are a human, you can think!

How many times have you been upset by a
bully or teaser? If you have been upset very many

times, this is the book for you! You no longer have to be somebody's victim and feel terrible . . . and you don't have to act like a bully or tease to protect yourself. In fact, you can turn someone else's annoying behavior into a game and have a good time. This book will tell you how.

If you were an animal instead of a person, bullies would be a problem. Animals have only two ways to act when they are threatened: They FIGHT or they FLEE. Because you are a human being you have a third choice: You can THINK! You can use your mind to figure out ways to stop the whole sorry business of teasing and to turn the worst bullies into buddies!

What Makes Teasers and Bullies Tick?

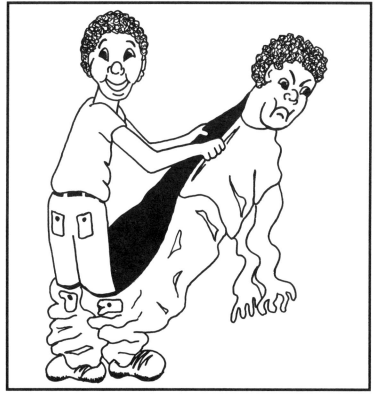

A person can get stuck inside a bully costume.

The first thing to THINK about is — what makes someone act like a pest or bully?

Bullies and Power

Bullies are not born that way. They are turned into young bullies by big bullies. Whenever you meet a bully, you can be sure there is or was a big bully lurking somewhere in his life. This big bully may have often made him feel weak or small. When a young bully bothers people, he may feel big and strong for a short time because he is upsetting others. But, when he remembers the big bully who hurt him, he feels sunk all over again.

When a person acts like a bully regularly, he starts to look like a bully. People say, "Oh, look, there's a bully!" They don't realize there is a person who has become stuck inside a bully costume.

Teasers and Attention

Teasers are not born that way either. They can turn into a tease from too little attention. Very few people receive all the attention they need or want. Most people would rather get their attention by being listened to and understood. When this kind of attention is hard to find, a person might settle for getting attention by making people angry.

Because it can be easier to make people angry than to find a good listener, some people get into a habit of teasing. Being a tease is a good way of getting bad attention.

Even though it doesn't feel good to have people angry at them, teasers get a lift by making people around them take notice. Then they end up feeling even worse because no one wants anything to do with them.

Teasers are like bullies. When they tease too much and too often, they start to look like a tease. But, you can always find a person stuck inside a tease.

General Meanness

Sometimes people act mean because they feel angry, hurt or afraid. They don't know how to put their feelings into words, so they act them out by doing and saying things to hurt other people. When someone is acting very angry, remember there is a sad, frightened person inside who isn't sure how to speak up.

3 Ways To Handle Bullies and Teasers

Now that you have thought about how people become teasers and bullies, you can put your mind on the next problem: If bullies and teasers are made by being hurt and ignored, what would be the best way to "un-make" them?

Suppose someone tells you, "Your mother wears combat boots." What could you do to talk person-to-person instead of bully-to-bully or bully-to-victim? Choose the best reply:

a. So what, your mother looks like a cow!

b. *I'm not surprised to hear that. She always has been a stylish woman.*

It doesn't take much thought to make the first reply. All you have done is imitate the bully — "monkey see, monkey do." The second reply takes human intelligence. It turns an insult into a compliment and talks to the person who has become stuck inside the bully.

1. Turning Insults Into Compliments

Any insult can be handled like a **COMPLI-MENT.** Ignore the bully's words and pretend he has said something nice. If you can't think of anything else to say, you can always say, *"Thank you."*

Bully: You're a real jerk.

Person: *Why, thank you. What a kind thing to say.*

Once you get used to taking things as a *compliment,* you can get quite clever.

Tease: Pizza face. (Said to someone with pimples.)

Person: *And I know you just love pizza!*

It's important to be persistent in your effort to turn rubbish into roses or the person stuck inside the bully may never get out:

Bully: Oh! You have kooties.

Person: *What a sweet thing to say. I didn't know you liked me so much.*

Bully: I don't like you. I can't stand you.

Person: *You can't fool me. If you didn't like me, you wouldn't always bother me.*

Taking meanness as a **COMPLIMENT** can also be called "speaking things as you want them." The funny thing is that when you do this, meanness often turns into the very thing you want it to be. After the person in the above example insisted the bully really liked her, he did, indeed, become her friend. At the very worst, a bully is likely to leave you alone when you take his attempts to clobber you as kindness.

Another way to turn an insult inside-out is to return it with a **COMPLIMENT**:

Bully: I must be smarter than you 'cause you're in that class for dumb people.

Person: *That's wonderful. The world needs all the smart people it can get.*

It is just about impossible to continue to be mean to someone who has just flattered you. But, if you've had a rough day and you just aren't quite up to using compliments, you can just say, "Why, thank *you. I'll take that as a real **comment**."*

Compliments can also be used to stop non-verbal meanness. If someone keeps poking you, you can say, *"I know you really have trouble keeping your hands off me. I guess I'm irresistible."* This puts you in a no-lose position. If they poke you again, you really are irresistible. If they stop, you achieved your goal.

Complimenting someone for their bad behavior and asking them to do it more can have the opposite effect. This is called "reverse psychology," or a **"REVERSER"** for short. Suppose someone burps in your face. You can say, *"You* *sure are a terrific burper. Let me hear you do that again."* Then keep asking her to burp some more until she begs to stop.

Reversers are really effective with insults. How would you use this technique if someone told you had dog breath? Compare your answer with the following:

> Excellent insult! Talk some more trash to me. I want to hear what else you can say with your razor sharp tongue.

REMEMBER: *Bullies expect insulting replies to their comments. They don't know what to do when they hear a compliment. While the bully is confused, the person inside of him has a chance to think.*

2. Asking Questions

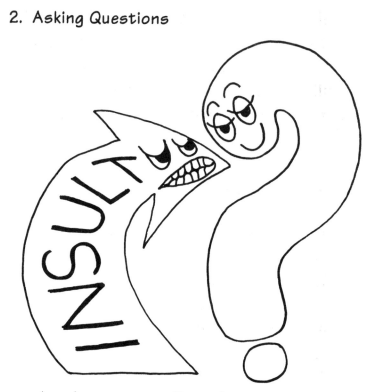

Another way to talk to the person inside the bully is to ask him **QUESTIONS.** Bullies and pests don't really think. They act out of habit. Questions make people think. Even if a bully won't answer your question, the person inside will probably be thinking about it. Thinking helps the person become stronger and weakens the bully.

In order to ask questions, just remember that many things bullies say and do don't make any sense. Get as curious as you can. Ask questions that will help you understand what the bully is trying to do:

Bully: You sure are ugly.
Person: *I guess that's your opinion, but why do you want to tell me that?*
Bully: 'Cause, I don't like you.
Person: *Well why do you want to talk to me if you don't like me? Why don't you just ignore me?*
Bully: Oh, just forget it!

Do you think the bully was able to make this person look bad? Was this person able to talk to the bully without using insults and acting like a bully himself? It is very hard to talk to a bully without acting like a victim or a bully yourself. Any time you can talk to a bully like a person, you score 10 points for helping stop the spread of meanness in the world!

REMEMBER: *People do not like to act mean or weak. They only do that when they are feeling too angry, hurt, or frightened to think of a better way to handle a problem.*

Read the next example. Do you think the person does a good job of helping to stop the spread of meanness in the world?

Tease: I bet you think all the boys at this skating rink are in love with you.

Person: *I'm glad you think I have so much confidence, but why are you bringing it up to me?*

Tease: 'Cause you think you're so hot.

Person: *Now I'm really confused. What's wrong with me feeling good about myself?*

Tease: It's not right to think you're better than everyone.

Person: *I certainly do agree with you. Do you think it's okay to think you're AS GOOD AS others?*

The person in this example didn't get tricked into defending herself and having a "No-I-don't-Yes-you-do" argument. By asking questions, she turned a possible spat into an interesting discussion. Generally, if you ask meanies questions long enough, you can find something good about what they are saying on which you can agree. This helps the person stuck inside the bully feel safe enough to come out.

Sometimes you may want to disagree with what a bully is saying. Don't! It just doesn't make any sense to disagree with nonsense. If you try to defend yourself, the bully might think he has said something true or important. This is called **"THE RULE OF BACKWARDS."**

> ***RULE OF BACKWARDS:*** *When you disagree with someone, it tends to make him think he is correct. When you try to understand the reason behind someone's thinking, it helps him consider other ideas.*

Ask questions that help you understand what a bully is trying to do.

3. Agreeing

If disagreeing with a bully makes him try to prove he is right, what do you think would happen if you **AGREE** with him? Could agreeing with someone make him have second thoughts about his ideas? What do you think happens in the examples below?

Bully: You are so stupid!

Person: *You mean I've been wasting all these years thinking I'm smart when I'm actually stupid. Thanks for wising me up!*

Person: *I've heard this song before.*

Bully: No, you haven't. You're lying.

Person: *Well, I thought I'd heard it before, but maybe I haven't.*

The bullies in these examples never get the satisfaction of starting an argument and upsetting someone. The person in each example says what he believes and quickly *acts* like he agrees with the bully. It's difficult to argue when someone is agreeing with you.

Bullies expect people to disagree with them. When someone agrees, they are surprised. They cannot use their old habits to strike back. Sometimes in this moment of confusion, meanies can begin to develop new habits.

Notice that the people in the examples don't actually agree that they are stupid or that they are lying. They agree with the *possibility* that they are not as smart as they thought or that they were mistaken. Even the silliest nonsense can be agreed with as a possibility:

> Tease: Your mother ate up all our cake.
> Person: *I've never known her to eat up other people's food, but anything is possible . . . Maybe we're not feeding well enough at home.*

Sometimes an insult is half nonsense and half true. You can always agree with the part that is true:

> Tease: You sure do take a bath with that hair spray.
> Person: *I do love to use it on my hair . . .*

Agreeing is one of the easiest ways to handle an insult. It can be so much fun to surprise a bully by agreeing with him, that other delightful ideas may pop into your mind:

> Person: *. . . Maybe I should start bathing in hair spray. I've never thought about what it would do for the rest of me.*

Very often a bully will take the truth and try to twist it into an insult. Eating sardines for lunch, religion, red hair — anything that is different, interesting or even pretty can become a target. Differences do not make one person any better or worse than anyone else. They just are! Agreeing with the facts and ignoring mean hints is the best way to untwist these insults and turn them back into the truth:

> Bully: Big nose!
> Person: *Why, yes, my nose is a bit large. How sweet of you to notice.*

Maybe I should start bathing in hair spray.

Golden Nuggets
and Prejudice

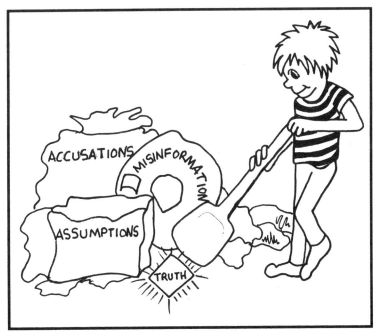

Find one little sparkle of goodness.

Some bullies have a very special weapon to make other people feel bad. It is called prejudice.

Prejudice means to judge a person before you know or understand what you are judging. Some people pre-judge anything that is different from themselves instead of trying to understand what makes others unique and special.

If a person doesn't feel good about himself, thinking he is better than people who are different from him can temporarily help him feel a little better. Many people have prejudices, but only a bully would use them as a weapon.

If someone tries to use prejudice as a weapon against you, keep asking questions until you can find one little sparkle of goodness in what he is saying with which to agree or compliment. That little sparkle is called a **GOLDEN NUGGET.** Pretend you are looking for a golden nugget:

Bully:	You black n_____!
Person	*I'm so glad you noticed that I'm black, but why are you going to so much effort to point out my race?*
Bully:	'Cause I don't like n_____s.
Person:	*What don't you like about black people?*
Bully:	You people are always pushing everyone around.
Person:	*Are you trying to make sure I don't push people around?*

Bully: Yeah . . .

Person: *I think it's great that you care so much about other people and want to protect them.*

Bully: Don't get smart with me.

Person: *I really mean it. I'm sure you have friends and family you care a lot about and you want to make sure that no one jumps them or gets the best of them.*

Bully: That's right! *(Looks puzzled and walks away.)*

It can be very tempting to defend yourself and others against prejudice. According to the rule of backwards, disagreeing with prejudice will only make someone more prejudiced. Showing interest in what a person thinks and finding something good to point out about his ideas interrupts prejudice by sneaking in the "back door" of a person's mind and making him feel good.

There is a kind of prejudice that can hurt your heart and your wallet. That's when people are seen as not as good as others because they can't afford to buy the "right" clothes, toys or cars. Even if you don't think you're concerned about how much money people have, you may be hooked on this nasty bit of judging when you start caring too much about yourself or your friends "fitting in." Watch how the person in the next example finds just the right **GOLDEN NUGGET** to keep this kind of prejudice from sneaking into a situation:

> Bully: What trash bin did you get your shoes from?
>
> Person: *(Looking confused) Hm . . . I just don't get it.*
>
> Bully: What?
>
> Person: *Why does someone like you, who has lots of friends and knows how to dress, care what I wear?*
>
> Bully: You don't fit in.
>
> Person: *That's so sweet of you to want to help me fit in! It's really sad the way some kids get left out because they can't buy the right stuff or aren't concerned about style.*

Even though you may be tempted to insult a bully for his silly thoughts, *don't*. This will only give the bully practice disagreeing and being mean back. Turning insults into **COMPLIMENTS,** asking **QUESTIONS, AGREEING,** and finding **GOLDEN NUGGETS** confuses a bully and helps the person inside of him get stronger.

Helping Others

Returning insults with compliments, asking questions, agreeing and combining these methods to find golden nuggets are your best defense against a bully.

Now that you have tools to use when someone is being mean to you, you may want to use them to help other people. That is excellent! Many young people want to do something to help fix the world's problems, but do not have the money, power or even voting rights to take action.

Turning bullies into people is something you can do right now! Even if someone goes back to being a bully, every minute he acts like a person counts. The thing to remember is to concentrate on helping the bully, even though you really want to help the victim:

Bully: *(To victim)* You Jew! I knew you wouldn't pay me my money.

Person: *Why are you complimenting her for not paying you your money? Jews are neat people. I'd be pretty angry if someone didn't pay me my money!*

The person in the above example turns an insult into a compliment, asks a question, and shows he understands the bully's feelings before the bully has a chance to use prejudice again. This works just as well with teasing. A bystander can turn an off comment into a golden nugget with very little effort:

Tease: *(To his sister)* I saw you with your boyfriend last night. I know you two were kissing.

Person: *Boy, you sure do love your sister! I never saw someone so worried about his sister's love life.*

2 More Methods for Handling Bullies

So far this book has given you four ways to handle insults and prejudice. When you are angry or hurt yourself, these methods may be hard to use. At times it can be best to just say what you are feeling or to show that you understand what the other person is feeling.

1. Express Your Feelings

Suppose that your sister brags that Aunt Rose bought her a pair of designer jeans. If you are feeling pretty good, you could use compliments or questions to make your sister's bragging less annoying:

—That's terrific. I know Aunt Rose really likes you a lot.
Are you just excited, or would you like me to turn green with envy?

However, if Aunt Rose is a sore spot with you, you might need to be honest and say how you are feeling:

Boy, am I jealous! Sometimes I think Aunt Rose likes you more than she does me and it hurts.

Many people are afraid to be honest with their feelings. They are afraid that if they let someone know they are sad or afraid, the other person will try to make them feel worse. Actually, the opposite is true. When one person can be honest with his feelings, it helps other people be more honest.

In the example above, as soon as one sister was able to say how she felt, the other was able to be more open:

I know what you mean. Grandpa seems to spend so much time with you and I feel left out.

Before they started being honest, these sisters spent a lot of time bragging and trying to make each other feel bad.

Being honest with your feelings can reach the human stuck inside of some of the worst bullies in this book. If someone is too angry after being called the "N-word" to look for golden nuggets, he could just say how he felt:

I can't stand it when white people use the "N-word." I'm really proud of my people and it hurts when someone doesn't like me because of my race. I wonder if anyone has ever said anything about you that you didn't like.

It might seem risky to be so honest with people who enjoy being cruel. As long as you are careful not to insult or criticize them in any way, the person inside the bully will probably hear you.

When you use the word "I" to say how you feel, it is not likely that you have used any insults. How many times did the person above use the word "I" to say his feelings? _____

The person above used the word "I" three

times to say his feelings. If he used the words "should" or "you," he would have been critical or insulting without even realizing it:

YOU SHOULDN'T talk that way. YOU make me sick. YOU wouldn't like it if someone called YOU names!

How many times did the person use the word "I" this time? It is impossible to say what you are feeling without using the word "I." In the above example, the person was stating his opinion and making an accusation.

Most people have a habit of using the words "should" and "you" instead of the word "I." They think they are saying their feelings when they are really being critical. Whenever you "should" someone, you are bound to get the same treatment in return. It is no wonder that people expect criticism and keep their guard up. It can be a very interesting experiment to say what you are feeling with the word "I" and find out how a person reacts.

If expressing feelings sounds a bit too serious for you, there is a way to add some fun to it and, possibly, win an acting award:

Bully: You look like you got your face

caught in a meat grinder.

Person: *(Starts to look tearful and bursts out crying.)*

Bully: Good grief! You don't have to be such a baby!

Person: *(In a pleasant voice) Well, I thought you wanted to hurt my feelings and I was only trying to be helpful.*

Grabbing your stomach and doubling over as though in pain is also a nice way to "help out" bullies when they try to inflict wounds with words.

2.   Feedback or Name Other People's Feelings

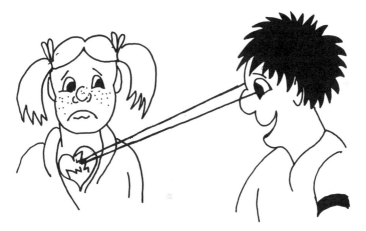

Not only is it important for you to say your feelings when you are too upset to think, it is important to help other people say their feelings when they are hurt or angry. When someone is both angry and a bully, you have to get through two layers to reach the person inside of him. You can usually tell by the tone of someone's voice if he is saying something just to be mean or if he is angry and hurt himself:

Bully: You know I could beat you to a pulp any time I want.

Person: *I don't blame you for being angry. Your team played a really good game of ball and it must not seem fair that my team won.*

Bully: Just shut up. I don't want to hear about your team.

Person: *Do you know how well you played?*

Bully: If we had played well, we would have won, stupid!

Person: *You sound even angrier at yourself than you do at me.*

Bully: (In spite of himself, the bully starts to get tears in his eyes.)

Person: *I know you always try your hardest and you usually do good. You're not used to making mistakes like I am.*

Bully: I can't stand losing!

Person: *Tell me about it . . .*

The hardest thing about helping someone say their feelings is to avoid telling him how he should feel. If the person above had tried to tell the bully not to be so hard on himself, he might have gotten popped in the eye. The kindest thoughts will not help when a person needs to be understood. By ignoring the bully's words and **FEEDING BACK** the feelings behind his comments, one person was able to help another say what was really hurting him.

Counselors go to special schools to learn how to help people say their feelings. They have to practice breaking old habits of giving advice and assuming they know what people feel. If you find it hard to understand what angry people are really feeling, it may be best to say as little as possible until someone can help you practice this kind of listening. Simply agreeing with this bully would have probably helped to calm him down, even if it did not get to the bottom of what was bothering him:

> Bully: You know I could beat you to a pulp any time I want?
>
> Person: *Believe me, I know you could! I've seen your strength.*

You do not have to wait to go to a special

school to learn to understand people when they are angry. Some people do this naturally. But, anyone can make the amazing discovery that he doesn't have to defend himself against angry people. Just remember that when people are angry they are not really thinking. They are feeling. Become as curious as you can and figure out what is making the person so upset:

> Bully: You stupid idiot. Why don't you watch where you're going instead of bumping into people!
>
> Person: *That really was quite a crash. I must have startled you.*
>
> Bully: You certainly did! How can you be so clumsy!?
>
> Person: *I know it's awfully upsetting when someone bumps into you . . .*

Even the angriest person will have difficulty carrying on with all this **UNDERSTANDING** and **SYMPATHY**. After awhile, the bully in the example above could be more startled by being understood than by being bumped. You will be surprised at how much more powerful you feel when you understand someone instead of defending yourself.

Some people make a habit of feeling angry.

Without realizing it they start expecting that other people will try to get the best of them, use them, or make them look foolish. A special kind of understanding is to **NAME THE FEELING** of suspicion, dissatisfaction, disappointment, or distrust in which a person has gotten stuck. It is especially powerful to use a question to name that feeling:

Bully: How could you be so stupid! Everyone knows what that word means.

Person: *Are you **disappointed** in me or my education?*

It is almost impossible for a bully to stay in the same feeling state when they get "caught in their act." Every time you help a person become aware of what he is doing, he can take a pause from his pattern and find some of the caring his anger has been keeping him from receiving:

Meanie: Get away from my things. What are you trying to do — rip me off!?

Person: *What happened to make you have such a hard time **trusting** people? I'd like to hear about it.*

Naming the feeling takes concentration. The

first step is to give other people permission to be upset with you. It's fine for you not to know or to forget to do something. If you really are being careless, understanding others will help you remember to do your best. But, everyone makes mistakes sometimes. When you stop feeling bad about yourself, you will be able to see the hurt in other people that causes them to get so angry. The strength you will find from stopping meanness by **NAMING** it, is really the power that comes form helping others.

*WARNING: There are times when a bully can be dangerous and want to hurt you physically. This is especially true if he has had something to drink or if he is showing off for a group. Do your best to avoid a bully who is acting this way. If you are unable to get away from him, say very little. Keep concentrating on what is making the bully so angry or mean. If a **QUESTION, AGREE-MENT, or UNDERSTANDING** comes to your mind, saying it might help calm the situation. However, do not push yourself to speak.*

Do's and Don'ts of Handling Insults and Teasing

Find out how well you understand what has been written so far. Put a check next to all the ways you can confuse a bully and help the person inside of him start thinking:

- ☐ Turn insults into **COMPLIMENTS**
- ☐ Return insults with **INSULTS**
- ☐ Give nice **EXPLANATIONS**
- ☐ **LECTURE** and **REASON**
- ☐ **DEFEND** yourself
- ☐ **AGREE** with possible truths
- ☐ **DISAGREE** with anything false
- ☐ Ask **QUESTIONS**
- ☐ Ask for more (**REVERSE** psychology)
- ☐ Give kindly **ADVICE**
- ☐ Say what you are feeling (**"I-STATEMENTS"**)
- ☐ State your **OPINIONS** ("You-Statements")
- ☐ Make **ACCUSATIONS**
- ☐ Show you **UNDERSTAND** what is upsetting a person
- ☐ Find something good to point out about what a person is thinking (**GOLDEN NUGGETS**)

As long as you only use **COMPLIMENTS, AGREE,** ask **QUESTIONS,** use **I-STATEMENTS, FEEDBACK** or **NAME FEELINGS,** use **REVERSE** psychology, and find **GOLDEN**

NUGGETS in what a bully is saying, you will be on the right track.

Bullies know just what to do with INSULTS, EXPLANATIONS, LECTURES, REASONS, DEFENDING, DISAGREEMENTS, ADVICE, OPINIONS, and ACCUSATIONS. They become very confused by almost anything else. You can be as creative as you want and develop your own style.

Advanced Techniques:

Here are a few more super duper ways to confuse a bully that are especially fun:

Bully: *(Yelling)* You can just go to h_ll!
Person: *(Yelling back) Well, you can just go to Disney World!*

Keeping your tone of voice the same as the bully's and using it to say something nice can be totally confusing and even make a bully crack a smile. These **"TONE TWISTERS"** are a good way to get out some of your frustration and stop an argument at the same time. Try it yourself. If a bully says, "Oh, shut up!," You can say, "_____" (See suggested answer on page 47.)

It's especially fun to use a tone twister to say something that is totally disconnected from the mean remark it follows. This can turn the I'm-not-your-friend nonsense that young children throw at each other into a game of sillies:

Meanie: *(In an angry voice)* I'm not your friend!

Person: *(Matching his anger) Well, I'm not your elbow!*

Meanie: *(Thinking)* Hmm, well, I'm not your guts.

Person: *(Smiling slightly) Well, I'm not your hair.*

Meanie: *(Smiling)* So, I'm not your toenail.

Person: *(Giggling) Okay, I'm not your tonsils . . .*

Older children can have just as much fun disconnecting from meanness:

Bully: Everyone is saying you go with all the boys.

Person: *Well, I heard that you're especially fond of dill pickles with your hamburgers.*

That puts rumors in a whole new light and throws a bully way off her track. When you use

DISCONNECTED COMMENTS you might get a funny look, or find yourself accused of being weird, but you are showing a bully that you are not going to take her nonsense seriously.

Speaking of being weird, don't ever miss an opportunity to play with that insult. Almost everybody gets told they are weird at some time in their lives. If you are ever given such an honor, simply hop on one foot, flap your arms like a bird and say, *"Do you really think so? . . . I always thought I was so normal."* You can get the same kind of mileage out of being told you're stupid:

> Bully: You're so ignorant! What's wrong with you?
>
> Person: *(Looking very puzzled) Ignorant? What does dat word mean?*

As long as a bully is going to call you a name, you might as well **"PLAY THE GAME."** Without using any words, you've said, *"I can handle being 'weird' or 'ignorant.'"* This gives the bully just the right dose of confusion to clear some meanness out of his or her mind. Think of how much fun it could be acting like you're crazy, a snob or a baby.

The last fun thing you need to know is the

magic of the words "try" and "dare." The word "try" **BLOCKS** someone from continuing whatever they are doing:

Person: *You can TRY to keep bothering me.*

The word "dare" has the opposite effect. It **PUSHES** people to reverse what they are doing or practice a new behavior:

Person: *I DARE you to be nice to me.*

With all this mental *blocking* and *pushing,* a bully can feel like his brain is getting fried and he won't be able to fight anything sensible you might want to say.

Now you have five advanced techniques of handling bullies: **TONE TWISTERS, DISCONNECTED COMMENTS, PLAYING THE GAME, BLOCKS** and **PUSHERS.** They are especially good for people who enjoy being silly or clever. Just thinking about using one of them will make you crack a smile. What bully will want to keep bothering you when his worst words only make you grin?

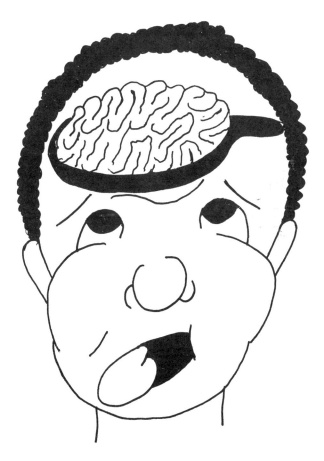

A bully can feel like his brain is getting fried.

—ANSWER FROM PAGE 43:
"Oh, go have a hot fudge sundae!"

Making Decisions
and Commitments

The object of this book is not to make you a
nice, kind person or to teach you to "turn the other

cheek." You have not even been advised to ignore name calling. Although that is not a bad idea, keeping quiet can be mistaken for hurt silence which does nothing to stop the spread of meanness.

Hopefully this book will remind you that you are a human being first! You were especially designed to think. You can use your mind to find solutions to problems. You now have enough information to make a decision. What is the best way to stop bullies, teasers and meanies from bothering you?

1. Fight fire with fire or gasoline. Think up meaner, more insulting things to say to bullies to try to make them stop bothering you.

2. Fight fire with water or sand. Think up ways to confuse bullies to the point where their "act" cannot work with you.

If you choose the first solution, watch out! Unless you really know what you're doing, fighting fire with fire can lead to bigger fires and pouring gasoline on a fire is sure to lead to an explosion.

If you made the second choice, have fun. The first time you turn an insult inside-out with **COMPLIMENTS, QUESTIONS, AGREEMENTS,**

FEEDING BACK/ NAMING FEELINGS, RE-VERSERS, TONE-TWISTERS, DISCON-NECTED COMMENTS, GAME-PLAYERS, BLOCKS or **PUSHERS,** you will be hooked. There may still be times when you'll get stuck, but that will only be when you are too upset to think clearly. You can figure out what you could have said when you are calmer. You will probably have a chance to use your idea later because bullies and teasers are not very clever and often repeat themselves.

Making a decision to "stop the spread of meanness" is one of the most important things you can do. Children are often mistreated by having too many decisions made for them; not being allowed to express their frustrations; being told their feelings are silly, unimportant or wrong; and in many other ways. Bullies are just passing on the disrespect they have felt themselves. They will never learn to stop unless someone shows them that there is another way! You can do this by changing the put-down/put-down or put-down/(hurt) silence "dramas" in which people get stuck. When you change the drama to **put-down/compliment, put-down/question** or any of the other fun ideas in this book, you will set people free!

After trying out some of the ideas in the book, you will know if taking on the "fight" against meanness is the right path for you. When you are ready to make this decision, you can start to put it into action with a **COMMITMENT:**

From this moment on I will do my best to treat all young people with complete respect, especially when they are acting their worst. I know I can do this by not taking meanness seriously and talking only to the good part of people with COMPLIMENTS, QUESTIONS, AGREEMENTS, REVERSERS, I-STATEMENTS, FEEDING BACK / NAMING FEELINGS, GOLDEN NUGGETS, TONE TWISTERS, DISCONNECTED COMMENTS, PLAYING THE GAME, BLOCKS and PUSHERS.

From this moment on I will do my best to . . .

A commitment is *not* a promise that you will always be respectful. It is a reminder that this is the way you want to act. It is designed to bring out all the reasons why you think you can't succeed. Read the above commitment and listen to any doubts that pop up in your mind . . .

Doubts are nothing more than old tape recordings that have gotten stuck in your brain and play very loudly. They may sound like — *"I'm not smart enough to do that . . ." "What if I want to be mean myself? . . ." "It might not work . . ."* You can quiet these recordings by saying them aloud with your nose pinched. Make them sound silly enough for you to hear a much quieter voice that is deep inside of you. It knows that you are good and that you can do whatever you set out to do!

If you have decided to join the fight against meanness, you will need to make your commitment over again every so often to air out your doubts and get you back in touch with the part of you that knows your strength. Each time you make your commitment, you get a fresh start and you have an unlimited supply of new beginnings.

Doubts are nothing more than old tape recordings . . .
you can hear a much quieter voice deep inside of you.

Practice

(For people who have decided to
join the fight against meanness.)

To show that you understand the ideas and
expressions used in this book fill in the blanks.

Answers are found on page 58.

1. Acting as if an insult were a _____ can be surprising and help turn a situation around. (p.15)

2. The best way to help someone consider new ideas is to _____ the reason behind his thoughts. The least effective way to help someone consider new ideas is to **DISAGREE** with him. This is called **"The Rule of Backwards."** (p. 21)

3. When you don't want to **AGREE** with what someone has said, you can always agree with the _____ that what she said is true. (p. 23)

4. Sometimes you may need to _____ _____ in order to **UNDERSTAND** why someone has said something mean. (pp. 18-21)

5. To use **REVERSE PSYCHOLOGY** ask someone to _____ doing something that is annoying you. This works because to keep from doing what you've asked him to do the bully has to stop. (p. 16)

6. To find **GOLDEN NUGGETS** you must keep asking questions until you can find a bit of _____ in someone's mean or silly words. (p. 26)

7. When you tell someone how his words or ac-

tions make you feel without using the word "should" you have made an _____-_____. (pp. 33-34)

8. Using **FEEDBACK, CONCERN** and **SYMPATHY** to show someone you_____ _____ him, helps him let go of any mean feelings. (pp. 35-38)

9. When you _____ the feeling state in which a person is stuck, you help her break the hold that feeling has on her. (p. 39)

10. When you use the word "should" to tell someone your feelings or thoughts, you are really giving advice, criticizing or making accusations. This is called "_____" someone. (p. 34)

11. When you use a **TONE TWISTER,** you use a mean tone of voice to say something _____. This is a good way to blow off steam, while adding humor to an argument. (p. 43)

12. When you make a comment that has nothing to do with what a bully has just said, you can _____ from any meanness that is coming your way. (p. 45)

13. Pretending to be whatever name you've been called makes the bully stop calling you that name in order to get you to stop **PLAYING THE** _____. (p. 45)

14. A powerful word that **BLOCKS** someone from continuing to do what they are doing is "_____." (p. 46)

15. A powerful word that **PUSHES** someone to reverse what they are doing or practice a new behavior is "_____." (p. 46)

ANSWERS: 1. compliment; 2. understand; 3. possibility; 4. ask questions; 5. continue; 6. truth and goodness; 7. I-statement; 8. understand; 9. name; 10. "shoulding;" 11. kind; 12. disconnect; 13. GAME; 14. "Try;" 15. "Dare."

Use **AGREEMENTS, COMPLIMENTS, QUESTIONS, I-STATEMENTS, FEEDBACK, NAMING FEELINGS, REVERSERS, GOLDEN NUGGETS, TONE TWISTERS, DISCONNECTED COMMENTS, PLAYING THE GAME, BLOCKS** or **PUSHERS** to respond to each situation below. There are many right answers. However, if you insult people, explain, disagree or defend yourself, you will not break the cycle of meanness. Several suggestions are given for each example on page 59.

1. Tease: Oh . . . you have freckles.

   Person: _____

2. Meanie: Boy, are you a sissy. You cry so easily.

   Person: _____ .

3. Bully: I'm glad I don't have a pig* for a father.
           (*police officer)

   Person: _____ .

4. Meanie: That boy you like told me he thinks you're
            fat and ugly.

   Person: _____ .

5. Bullies: A gang of 12-year-olds see a fort that a
             10-year-old is building and destroy it.

   Person: _____ .

6. Tease: Your lunch looks like vomit.

   Person: _____ .

7. Meanie: You Blockhead! How could you be so ir-
            responsible?!

   Person: _____ .

Suggested Responses

1. Tease: Oh . . . you have freckles.

   Person: **—You're so right (AGREEING)**
            —I'm so glad you noticed . . . but the
            question is, how many? (Taking an in-
            sult as a COMPLIMENT)
            —Well, your skin is just beautiful! (Re-

turning an insult with a COMPLI-
MENT)
—I know, but please don't tell anyone.
I'm trying to pass for clear skinned.
(Humor)
—Water, water everywhere and not a
drop to drink. (DISCONNECTED
COMMENT)

2. Meanie: Boy, are you a sissy. You cry so easily.
   Person: —That's true. I do cry easily. (AGREE-
   ING)
   —How nice of you to notice what a sen-
   sitive, feeling person I am. (Taking an
   insult as a COMPLIMENT)
   —I'll be glad to teach you. I hear cry-
   ing prevents ulcers. (Taking an insult as
   a COMPLIMENT))
   —Do you really think it's bad to cry?
   (Asking a QUESTION)
   —I know. I like to please people and I
   really feel hurt when someone is disap-
   pointed in me. (I-STATEMENT)
   —(Whining loudly) Do you really think
   I'm a sissy? (PLAYING THE GAME)

3. Bully: I'm glad I don't have a "pig" for a father.
   Person: —What do you mean? Do you dislike
   cops? (Asking a QUESTION)
   —Some police officers can be pretty
   rough. (AGREEING)

—Thanks for the sympathy. You must understand how much I worry about my father getting hurt. (Treating an insult as a COMPLIMENT)

4. Meanie: That boy you like told me he thinks you're fat and ugly.

   Person: —Ouch! That hurts. (I-STATEMENT)
   —Are you trying to hurt my feelings or trying to be my friend? (Asking a QUESTION)
   —How good of you to tell me . . . I guess you don't want me to make a fool of myself. (Finding a GOLDEN NUGGET)
   —You do an excellent job of making sure I find out about any bad comments people say about me. (COMPLIMENT)
   —I dare you to tell me something nice. (PUSHER)

5. Bullies: A gang of 12-year-old bullies see a fort that a 10-year-old is building and destroy it.

   Person: —Doesn't say anything and leaves the area as quickly as possible because he knows he is out-numbered.
   —The next day the 10-year-old sees the leader of the gang alone and says, "I bet you had a good time wrecking my fort. Sometimes it makes me feel good to mess up my sister's stuff and make her mad. (Showing UNDERSTANDING)

—The 10-year-old asks his parents for help and the next day they arrange to talk with the bully and his parents.

6. Bully: Your lunch looks like vomit.

   Person: —**Well, it's a fresh crop from this morning's bed pan. (Pretending to AGREE)**
   —**That just makes me want to hurl for sure — you'd better get out of my way, I really spew! (PLAYING THE GAME.)**
   —**I never realized you were so concerned about my health. (Taking it as a COMPLIMENT)**

7. Meanie: You Blockhead! How could you be so irresponsible!?

   Person: —**It really wasn't right of me to be late. (AGREEING with the part that is true)**
   —**This must have been very difficult for you. (UNDERSTANDING)**
   —**I'm so sorry. What hardships did I cause? (Asking a QUESTION)**
   —**I'm sure you feel just furious (NAMING THE FEELING)**

Notice how examples five and seven are different from the others. Example five is a situation that could be dangerous. The person may need help from adults to handle it. In example seven the "meanie" is really upset. When people are angry, it is best to use techniques that show understanding and help release feelings. Humorous and clever comments should be saved for name calling and general nonsense.

REMEMBER: *There are many right answers. Everyone has their own style. In each example, which suggested response makes you feel most comfortable?*

Turning Ideas into Action

People accidentally pick up bad habits by re-
peating a behavior over and over without thinking

about what they are doing. You can train yourself to develop just the habits you want by concentrating on what you are doing.

The Anti-Meanness Chart on the following page can help you. It breaks the "anti-meanness" habit into three steps:

1) **Not returning meanness with meanness;**
2) **Using the ideas in this book to interrupt meanness;**
3) **Thinking about a situation after it happens when you have not been able to figure out what to do at the time.**

The last step is so important that even when you act like a bully yourself, you still get some credit if you can figure out what you could have said differently later.

Each step is worth points. You can earn three or more points a day while you are training yourself in the anti-meanness habit. Just turning your efforts into points will help you concentrate on what you are doing and make you want to keep trying.

Parents are great people to help you learn new habits. They may be willing to give you rewards for earning "anti-meanness" points. Every day you just give your parents a report of what you've done to stop the spread of meanness and they give you credit on the Anti-Meanness Chart. To earn points for steps two and three, you have to tell your parents what you said to stop meanness or what you could have said. Not only will you help yourself, but you may help your parents. They have to put up with a lot of meanness from other adults.

ANTI-MEANNESS CHART

Name: _____

Anti-Meanness Steps	M	T	W	T	F	S	S
1. I did not use INSULTS, ARGUMENTS, "SHOULDS," ACCUSATIONS or EXPLANATIONS to handle meanness today. (5 points)							
2. I was able to handle someone's meanness with COMPLIMENTS, QUESTIONS, AGREEMENTS, GOLDEN NUGGETS, I-STATEMENTS, UNDERSTANDING, REVERSERS, TONE-TWISTERS, DISCONNECTS, GAME PLAYERS, BLOCKS, PUSHERS or HUMOR. (5 points)							
3. When I got stumped by meanness, I was able to figure out what I could have said later. (5 points)							
4, No meanness came my way today.; I must be doing something right. (3 points)							
TOTAL:							

Rewards: _____

_____

_____

Partners and Clubs

A habit is easier to learn when you work on it with someone else. If you and a friend decide to join the fight against meanness together, you can think up ways to reward each other for points earned. You can treat your friend to a snack or let him borrow a record of yours for a week when he earns 70 points.

There are times when it really helps to have a partner to take on the cruelty in the world. Suppose you and your friend overhear a nasty bit of prejudice. A white girl is telling a black girl, *"I don't want help from no black person!"* One of you can start using **GOLDEN NUGGETS** by saying, *"Gosh, I had no idea it isn't cool to get help from black people! Tell me where you got that thought from."*

The other person can take the black girl aside so she doesn't have to hear any more vicious viewpoints. A comment like, *"Isn't it sad that some white people don't know how fine black people are?"* can help make the situation clear so it doesn't get muddied by hurt and anger.

You can even start an anti-meanness club. At meetings you can take turns telling comments members made to blow off "word waste" with "word wit." Club members can vote on each comment to see if it passes the anti-meanness test:

ANTI-MEANNESS TEST

1. Comment does NOT use any INSULTS, PUT-DOWNS, ADVICE, DISAGREEMENTS, "SHOULDS," "YOU-STATEMENTS," ACCUSATIONS, LECTURES, OPINIONS or EXPLANATIONS to handle meanness.
2. Comment does use COMPLIMENTS, QUESTIONS, AGREEMENTS, GOLDEN NUGGETS, I-STATEMENTS, FEEDBACK, REVERSERS, TONE-TWISTERS, DISCONNECTS, GAME-PLAYERS, BLOCKS, PUSHERS or HUMOR to handle meanness.

Anyone who got stumped by meanness can explain the situation and have the club figure out a clever way to have turned the situation around. Each week one person can renew his or her anti-meanness commitment (see page 52) and air out his self-doubts by saying them to the club in the silliest possible way. Then the club can come up with an opposite way for him to say his "doubt:"

Doubt: What if I can't do it? *(Said in a whiny voice)*

Opposite: What if I can do it? *(Said in a calm, curious voice)*

Doubt: I can't let anyone get the best of me! *(Said with a mean, ugly look and voice)*

Opposite: It's possible I could let someone THINK they got the best of me. *(Said with a casual, thoughtful voice)*

Doubt: I'm scared to try something new. *(Said with a worried voice and facial expression)*

Opposite   I'm scared to try something new.
Tone: *(Said cheerfully to twist the tone)*

Don't be surprised if turning self-doubts inside-out creates a lot of giggles, groans and even some tears. Just keep it up until the person starts to hear her "still small voice" that knows her true ability!

When a group of people gets together to tackle a problem, the power they create can be awesome. There is a natural "high" that comes from being a knight for niceness. Clubs can take on special projects to transform a particular bully with sympathy, kindness and cleverness. They can create a safe place for someone to share the problems of daily dealings with a sour parent or a bossy sister. Anyone who is serious about helping kids help kids should be allowed to join an "anti-meanness club!"

Final Vision

You can feed a starving world.

Once someone had a dream of a table filled with the most delicious food imaginable. Many people were seated on both sides of the table but no one was eating. Everyone had long forks and spoons growing out of their arms that made it impossible to reach their own plates. They were wildly trying to grab food from any dish they could and find some way of cramming it into their mouths. This was very difficult because the spoons and forks growing out of their arms were so long that they often missed their mouths or jabbed themselves.

Things became more chaotic. There was much shouting, groaning and drooling but no one was getting fed. Was there any solution?

In spite of her hunger, one person decided she would no longer take part in this absurd feeding frenzy. She rested her arms at her sides and looked at the situation. Then an idea came to her. Carefully she used one of her spoon-arms to get some food from one of the most delicious-looking platters and offered it to someone else. This was not hard because many people's mouths were in easy reach of her long arms. The person she fed was able to relax enough to grasp the situation and, he too, began feeding others.

It took awhile, but eventually the table was filled with happy, satisfied people, feeding each other and making soft murmurs of contentment. Some people were quick to understand and easily made the change from being takers to givers. Others needed a lot of feeding before they were brave enough to stop guarding their own plates or trying to grab from others.

And you, my dear reader, what about you? Have you rested enough to read this book and **understand what is happening?** How long will it take you to **stop guarding your pride or trying to take strength from others?** Have you discovered what it is like to **empower yourself without overpowering anyone?** Do you know now that there is a deep well of humor, honesty, understanding and love inside of you that can feed a "starving" world? You will find it soon enough and take your turn in the chain reaction that can save us from ourselves.

*G*lossary of Anti-Meanness Terms

ACCUSATION: Statement blaming someone for a wrong doing. *Encourages people to make counter accusations.*

ADVICE: A statement which recommends a course of action for another person. *Implies that the other person needs to change and will encourage the other person to disagree or defend himself.*

AGREEMENT: Statement that agrees with or accepts what someone has said as correct, possibly correct or generally true. *Makes it difficult for someone to carry on an argument or disagreement.* (p. 22)

BLOCKS: A statement or word like "try" which *discourages someone from continuing to do what they are doing.* (p. 46)

COMPLIMENT: Statement which praises or points out something good. Can be used as though an insult were a compliment to "SPEAK IT AS YOU WANT IT" or to return an insult with a compliment. *Very unexpected response to an insult which* *tends to stop an argument or turn around a situation.* (p. 14)

DISAGREEMENT: Statement which finds fault with or points out the errors in what someone has said. *Encourages further disagreement from other people.*

DISCONNECT: Statement that is unrelated to the one it follows. Non sequitur. *Such statements help a person emotionally disconnect from the previous comment.* (p. 45)

EXPLANATION: A statement which attempts to make clear, give REASONS or DEFEND one's actions. *Encourages others to find fault and argue with what is being said.*

FEEDING BACK FEELINGS: A statement which shows UNDERSTANDING by rephrasing what a person is thinking or feeling. UNDERSTANDING can also be shown by expressing CONCERN, COMPASSION, SYMPATHY, and INTEREST in another person's experience. *Helps people release and let go of angry feelings that cause mean comments.* (p. 37)

GAME PLAYERS: Acting out or dramatizing the very insult a person has been called. (Comes from the expression, "Give me a name and I'll play a game.) *Can make a person take back an insult to make the drama stop.* (p. 45)

GOLDEN NUGGET: A technique in which a person keeps asking questions until she can find a little sparkle of truth or goodness to compliment in the mean things another person has been saying. *Can help a bully identify with the good part of himself instead of the mean part.* (p. 25)

HUMOR: Statement that contains something absurd, silly, ridiculous or out of place that makes a situation less serious and heavy. *Shows that little importance should be placed on mean comments.*

INSULT: A statement which causes hurt feelings or deep resentment. *Will usually cause other person to make counter insult sooner or later.*

I-STATEMENT: A statement beginning with the word "I" that tells how a person feels in a particular situation. *Discourages* *arguments because it is harder to disagree with feelings than with thoughts.* (p. 33)

LECTURE: A series of statements which criticize, scold or advise someone how they should conduct themselves. *Often creates resentful silence or further disagreement.*

NAMING FEELINGS: A special kind of FEEDBACK which labels the feeling state in which a bully has gotten stuck. *Naming a feeling usually breaks the hold it has over a person.* (p. 39)

OPINION: A belief or judgment stated as though it were a fact. *Often used to imply that others are wrong which encourages arguments.*

PUSHER: A statement or word like "dare" which *pushes a person to reverse what they are doing or practice a new behavior.* (p. 46)

PUT-DOWN: See INSULT.

QUESTION: A request for further information. *Helps a person focus on understanding something they don't like instead of disagreeing with it.* (p. 18)

REVERSER: A request that an uncooperative person do just what she is doing in order to help her do the opposite. *Pushes a bully to change her behavior in order to remain uncooperative.* (p. 16)

SHOULDS: A statement containing the word "should" which implies that another person is wrong or at fault. *Encourages other people to disagree and defend themselves.*

TONE-TWISTER: A statement which uses a mean tone of voice to say something nice. *Helps release frustrations without using insults and adds confusion to make a situation less serious.* (p. 43)

YOU-STATEMENT: A statement that begins with the word "YOU" that tells what one person thinks of another. *May cause the other person to defend herself or counter-attack.*

Information for Parents

When children have frequent arguments and fights, parents often have difficulty deciding what their role should be. They may be concerned that their child is bad or weak, or they may be puzzled that their child fights at all.

Why Children Fight

Peer fighting is actually an important part of growing up. Children are learning how to negotiate conflicts with people their own age. This is a much different task than handling conflicts with adults.

Even toddlers will fight. However, turmoil among children increases in the middle of the fourth grade and continues through junior high school. This is the gang age. Children are making a transition from the importance of parents as the primary figures in their lives to a world where love and acceptance are less certain. They must compete with their peers as they learn to be workers and acquire the skills of adult life. In this task children are constantly vulnerable to feelings of inferiority. Winning battles and feeling "better than" gives brief relief from fears of failure.

By the time young people enter high school, there is generally some decrease in peer fighting. When problems do continue, conflicts can be particularly vicious and even dangerous. Outside help may be needed for particularly aggressive or meek children.

The Parent's Role

For the most part, the seemingly cruel world of fighting, teasing and name calling must be the child's battleground. Parents should do little more than help their children "lick their wounds" and understand the forces with which they are dealing. The ideas in this book can be used as information, rather than as advice:

When you call other people names, you are likely to be

called names in return. What ideas in the book you read on bullies could you have used instead?

In situations where there is a threat of real danger, parents do need to take charge. The example on page 61 suggests that adult involvement can provide the support children need to safely confront each other. Adults can be especially effective if they use ideas in this book to manage such confrontations. When one child is clearly at fault, the parents of both the victim and the bully need to create an atmosphere in which the aggressor can take time to think about his actions:

> You are a good child. So, what were you thinking when you tore down that fort? Were you angry yourself or did you think it was a way of looking tough?

Even though children may have difficulty answering these questions, they will be hearing an important message — *"I am good in spite of my behavior and I can learn to make changes."* The aggressor can also be encouraged to evaluate his actions:

> Are you proud of what you did? What was good about how you handled that? What was bad? Do you know how Johnny felt when you destroyed his fort? Have you ever felt that way? Tell me about it.

Finally, adults can impose consequences for destructive behavior which are a vital part of a child's learning:

> You will not be able to ride your bike or watch TV until you have rebuilt Johnny's fort.

The parent's main goal should not be to punish the aggressor. Bullies are punished over and over, and later they pass punishments on to those who are smaller than themselves. If the parents of the victim make it their first priority to UNDERSTAND the aggressor, his own parents will be less likely to be overly defensive and punitive. Generally, it is up to the aggressor's parents to decide what corrective action is needed. However, in serious cases involving assaults or property damage, it may be important for the victim's parents to take legal action.

Sometimes parents need to interrupt a dangerous situation when it is not clear who is the victim and who is the aggressor. Although each child will want support for his or her side, parents should not take the role of judge. Instead, adults can listen to each child to understand what is upsetting him or her without finding fault. Then the children involved can be required to make a statement showing they understand what the other person is feeling before they continue with their activities. Anytime children's bickering starts to annoy parents, they can use this approach.

Although it is important for parents to maintain some distance from young people's conflicts, they do not have to stand by helplessly while their child is in pain. The *"Anti-Meanness Chart"* on page 68 is an excellent vehicle for parents to use to help young people learn to navigate the turbulent waters of childhood and adolescence.

The *Anti-Meanness Chart* is especially effective in reducing name calling between siblings because it creates a reverse psychology. Being called a name takes on a whole new meaning when it creates an opportunity for a child to earn points on his or her chart. Simply saying, *"Thanks for helping me earn points,"* is worth five points in itself. Parents can also make a rule that anyone in the family who gets hit, shoved or pushed earns a "victim's compensation point." Then an annoying brother or sister can be told, *"Thanks for the poke . . . that will earn me six points* (five points for saying, "Thank you" plus one victim's compensation point) *towards my next bag of chips."* To avoid tattling, children earn points when they ONLY tell what they did to help a situation (not who did what wrong). In one family just knowing that aggravating someone else would help him or her almost completely eliminated fighting.

Afterword and Acknowledgment

My head is full of books to write, but **Bullies and Teasers** will always be my most important work. It is the fruit of my own early struggles. Although my family wasn't perfect, any shortcomings my parents had were no match for the cruelty I met from my age-mates. Perhaps, the very gentleness of my own home left me without a tough hide to protect myself from the meanness that lay beyond my door. For many years I was very sensitive to any hurts that came my way.

Gradually, I discovered a secret. My first clue came in the sixth grade when my mother told me to tell a boy who had been tormenting me that I knew he just wanted to be my friend . . . and guess what? Overnight, he did become my friend. I was most grateful but had no idea what *hadn't* hit me.

I continued to have more growing pains until my senior year in high school. My friends, out of their own ignorance, were using my religion to insult other people. One day a compliment popped out of my mouth putting my religion in the good light it deserved. The power I felt from that one little comment and the leap in my self-confidence made me stand up and take notice.

I began to analyze what I was doing and to look for other challenges on which to sharpen my new-found skills. Every time I discovered a new way to "recycle" the verbal garbage that came my way, my sense of confidence and power took another giant step. Particular incidents are etched in my mind . . . there was the time when I playfully handled one of my father's silly temper tantrums by asking him if he was disappointed in me or my education. Another night I calmly sympathized with the difficult spot I had left a doctor in while he yelled at me for being irresponsible and I killed his outburst with compassion.

By the time I was a therapist I knew well how to be assertive. However, I realized my moments of empowerment were going far beyond standing up for myself. I wasn't telling others what I was feeling, wanting or willing or not willing to do.

I was focused entirely on the other person or the situation — whether that be the misguided efforts of a sixth grade boy to be friendly; my friends' misinformation about my religion; my father's absurd standards for intelligence; or a frazzled doctor's efforts to make his emergency room run like a well-oiled clock. I discovered the power of seeing through others. This freed me to flex my mind and give a healing touch to the part of the "picture" that needed adjusting.

I don't believe that great discoveries are made independently and I certainly am not the only one who knows how to massage the trouble spots in knotty situations. I made it my hobby to seek out others who were on my mission and learned from them.

My greatest source of wisdom came from Re-evaluation Counseling (RC). RC is a peer counseling movement that has made a study of the ways people systematically hurt each other in socially acceptable ways. Finding **GOLDEN NUGGETS,** using **TONE TWISTERS** to interrupt mean patterns, exaggerating self-defeating patterns to scorn them, and making **COMMITMENTS** all come from the body of knowledge this brilliant lay counseling movement has amassed.

The language of hypnosis offered further tools to help me refine my skills. Hypnosis is the gentle art of moving a person from one mental state to another through language. Hypnosis uses **BLOCKS** to tell people they can "try" to keep their eyes open or **PUSHERS** to "dare" people to get all the way relaxed. One of the masters of hypnosis, Milton Erickson, used **DIS-CONNECTS,"** or non sequiturs, to confuse people enough to accept healthy suggestions. Erickson also used **"REVERS-ERS"** (paradoxical suggestions) which encourage people to continue doing anything that resists trance in order to help them slip into one.

I-STATEMENTS and **UNDERSTANDING** (active listening) are standard communication training. Although it is the intention of the anti-meanness method to go beyond these skills, there is always a place for direct communication and times when it is essential. Psychology often places special importance on sending assertive **I-STATEMENTS.** The gentle art of **UNDER-**

STANDING, SYMPATHIZING, and showing CONCERN and INTEREST may be far more powerful in helping people ultimately get what they want. Most recently, the best selling book, **The Celestine Prophecy,** points out how labeling feelings or "NAMING the drama," completely changes interaction between people and prevents one person from trying to "feed off" another's energy.

I first encountered the technique of AGREEING with any truth, possible truth or true principle behind incoming criticism in the book, **When I Say No, I Feel Guilty,** by Manual J. Smith, Ph.D., 1980. Mr. Smith's book empowers by teaching an attitude that helps people stop feeling guilty so they can *listen* for any grains of truth in other people's distress.

I am not sure where my use of COMPLIMENTS comes from. It seems to be the easiest technique and the heart of the anti-meanness method. It has a touch of RC because it overlooks oppressive patterns and concentrates on the good person underneath; and it is hypnotic because it predicts what can happen. Some psychologists would say COMPLIMENTS are a way of "reframing" an insult as something nice. Telling someone who has just made a nasty remark that she has such a clever way of being kind can almost seem like sarcasm or a lie unless it is said in a sincere tone of voice. A client gave the best understanding of COMPLIMENTS when she told me in her church they call this approach SPEAKING THINGS AS YOU WANT THEM. I do believe that taking insults as COMPLIMENTS forms the spiritual core of the anti-meanness method. It puts into action the principle that IT IS A GREATER SIN TO TAKE OFFENSE THAN TO GIVE OFFENSE.

Finally, the source of PLAYING THE GAME eludes me. I think it, indeed, comes from playing. My daughter and I happened upon it one night while giving her a bath. Therefore, I give her full credit for PLAYING THE GAME as she endeavors to take the **Bullies and Teasers** approach into new frontiers where no one has been before.

About the Author

Kate Cohen-Posey, M.S. LMHC LMFT has been a therapist practicing in Polk County, Florida, since 1973. The literature she has written for clients over the years has provided a medium for artistic expression of her therapeutic skills. The popularity of her writing with clients and colleagues has encouraged her to reach a wider audience. It is her aim to develop concise, easy-to-read materials that assist and shorten the therapeutic process OR provide a means of independent study for those who wish to further their own emotional / spiritual development.

How to Handle Bullies, Teasers, and Other Meanies

For additional copies of *How to Handle Bullies, Teasers, and Other Meanies*, contact the distributor, Book Clearing House, at telephone (toll free) 1-800-431-1579, facsimile (914) 835-0398, email: BookCH@aol.com, www.BookCH.com. All major credit cards are accepted.

Bulk discounts of this book are available, and such purchases may be arranged through the publisher, Rainbow Books, Inc., P. O. Box 430, Highland City, FL 33846-0430, telephone (863) 648-4420, email: rbibooks@aol.com